A Message of Inspiration for the Graduate

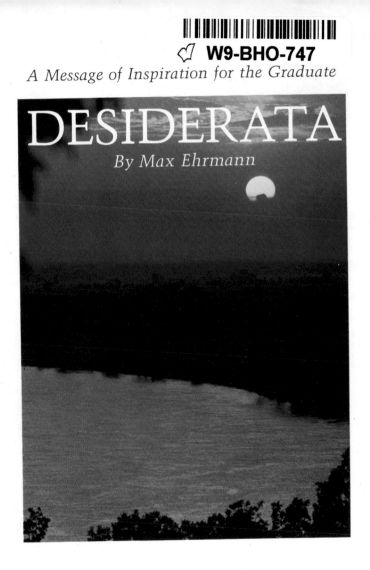

# DESIDERATA
## By Max Ehrmann

*G*o placidly amid
the noise and the haste,
and remember what peace
there may be in silence.

*As far as possible without surrender be on good terms with all persons. Speak your truth quietly and clearly; and listen to others, even the dull and ignorant; they too have their story.*
*Avoid loud and aggressive persons, they are vexations to the spirit.*

*If you compare yourself
with others you may become
vain and bitter; for always
there will be greater and lesser
persons than yourself.*

*E*njoy your achievements
as well as your plans.
Keep interested in your own
career, however humble;
it is a real possession in the
changing fortunes of time.

*Exercise caution in your
business affairs; for the world
is full of trickery. But let this
not blind you to what virtue
there is; many persons strive
for high ideals; and everywhere
life is full of heroism.*

*Be* yourself.
Especially do not feign affection.

Neither be cynical about love;
for in the face of all aridity
and disenchantment it is as
perennial as the grass.

*Take* kindly the counsel of the years, gracefully surrendering the things of youth.

*Nurture strength of spirit to shield you in sudden misfortune. But do not distress yourself with imaginings. Many fears are born of fatigue and loneliness.*

Beyond a wholesome discipline,
be gentle with yourself. You are
a child of the universe no less
than the trees and the stars;
you have a right to be here.
And whether or not it is clear to
you, no doubt the universe is
unfolding as it should.

*T*herefore be at peace with God, whatever you conceive Him to be, and whatever your labors and aspirations, in the noisy confusion of life keep peace with your soul.

With all its sham, drudgery and broken dreams, it is still a beautiful world.

*Be* careful.
*Strive to be happy.*